We Might Win
or
We Might Lose

Bill Franklin
Illustrated by Nina Mkhoiani

Niche Publishing Co. Llc
Bill Franklin Books
Colorado Springs, USA

For

Liam

and

Ainsley

Thanks to Nina Mkhoiani, "Sylvanaz" on Fiverr.com, for the excellent illustrations in this book.

Amazon.com Book Link:
https://www.amazon.com/dp/1725040476/

Niche Publishing Co, Llc
Bill Franklin Books
PO Box 62114
Colorado Springs, CO 80962-2114

Printed in USA

Would you like to give your children free coloring pages of the illustrations in this book?

To instantly receive a free PDF with full-size coloring pages of each image, just use the internet link on the last page.

And please consider taking just one moment to leave your opinion of the book on Amazon. Just go to bit.ly/WinLoseReviews. Thanks!

Happy Reading! ... Bill Franklin

Donovan was on the very best team in his soccer league, but they were just not ready for the team they played today! He was having great fun on the field until he looked up and saw the score. They had lost the game!

Have *you* ever played in a game before

And you weren't on the team that won?

... Then when you saw the final score

It took away all of your fun?

Of course, the fans on the sidelines weren't happy about it either—especially his sister, Julie, who had lost her own softball game the day before! This was a bad week for both of them!

Someone is certainly going to win

And someone else will lose.

... That's just how it's always been

You don't usually get to choose!

Their dad always had something helpful to say. Even when they didn't win, he could make them laugh! Like today, he made up a rhyme about being a ball getting hit hard by a bat! And then he told them one about a huge tree being cut down by one man! Just imagine how *they* felt! (If they *could* feel things, that is!)

**'Cause sometimes we feel
like the baseball bat,**

**Or we might be
whacked like the ball!**

Or we might be the lumberjack

Who makes a mighty tree fall!

Then Donovan's little brother, Timmy, said, "Aw, Dad, we're just *kids*! We're not balls or trees!" Their dad laughed out loud and agreed with him that he was certainly *not* a tree!

Of course, boys and girls
aren't balls or trees—

You try hard to win every game...

But the way it always works, you see:

All the *others* are doing the same!

Dad even talked about something they were all involved with, except Timmy: SCHOOL! He said, "You don't give up after a low grade, do you?"

Sometimes you'll get a pretty good grade,

(Though someone else's is better.)

But you can be sure, that memory will fade.

Next time *you'll* get that "A" letter!

Then their dad told them that it's important to be a "good sport." He called it "good
sportsmanship," and it seemed to mean not
taking a game too seriously, even though they
should try hard to win every time.

For it's not just about if
you win or lose—

An *extremely* important fact.

The end might not be the
one you choose,

But it matters, how you act!

H e also said it was always okay to win a game or a race, but even when we win, we should always remember to be nice to others!

> And when you win,
>   it's *okay* to grin
>
> And show how happy you are.
>
> It's all right to show
>   the great mood you're in,
>
> For the winner is *always* the star!

Donovan said, "A kid on the other team last week started crying after we beat them!" Dad said, "Yes, some young people get very upset when they lose. But it's usually better not to cry in front of your teammates."

So when you find
    you've lost a game,

        You might not hear
            the crowd's cheers.

But if you played hard,
    don't *ever* feel shame.

        And for sure,
            don't shed any tears!

After they drove for awhile, their dad said, "You know, one of the good things about sports is that you get to play again! One game doesn't make the whole season, does it?" The kids all agreed with him.

'Cause there's always
another game to play

Or a contest you can win.

Don't let not winning
mess up your day.

Just go out and try again!

Donovan spoke up and said, "And, I made friends with a boy on the other team, even though they beat us!" They all laughed together.

Losing a game you want to win

  Will happen to you someday.

But if you can do it and keep a grin

  You'll feel better in every way!

Julie had not said very much yet. Now she spoke up. "But, Dad, it's just a *pain* when someone else is *so* good they always win!" He answered, "Yeah, but that *could* be you, right? And it's still okay to win a lot."

But what if you win
again and again ...

Because you are *really good?*

It's *always* okay
for you to win!

Just be a good sport,
like you should!

Dad said, "It's a funny thing about people watching sports. They often like the person best who is the best sport. Being humble and not gloating—that's what crowds like."

It's not just the strongest
    or fastest one

    Who wins
        the crowd's embrace.

... not just the person who
    had the best run,

    But the one who
        shows the most grace.

Dad continued, "The main thing to remember is that you should just always do your best. That's all you can do!"

So, if it's first place we
want to earn ...

If we want to be
champion someday.

Here's the lesson we all
have to learn —

Do our best, every
time we play!

"Yeah," Julie said. "I try my best but we *still* get beat!" Dad answered, "I know, Jules—that's just what it's like in sports. But keep working hard. You'll eventually win!"

**Sometimes you play
your *very* best ...**

**But the other team
wins by a mile!**

**It's *still* okay!
There's another contest**

And *you* can end up with a smile.

Donovan said, "Yeah, Julie! You were third place in cross country last year, but this year you were *first!*" Julie just laughed and nodded yes.

'Cause it's always true for everyone

That someone else
might do better

But the more you grow,
the *faster* you'll run

Then *you* will be the pacesetter!

You won't be the winner
in every game.

What you've learned in
this book is true.

But always do your best,
just the same.

It will make you
a happier you!

So don't *ever* give up,
and *never* give in,

In everything you do!

Soon *you* will wear
the winner's grin —

THE CHAMPION WILL BE YOU!

Dad stopped the car at their house. Then he looked at all of them and said with a big smile: "You guys are *all* winners in my book! Let's go grill some hamburgers!"

Resources for Parents

The following websites and articles can be helpful as you explain the realities of winning and losing to your children.

https://www.healthline.com/health-news/children-should-play-more-than-one-sport

https://experiencelife.com/article/putting-kids-and-fun-back-into-kids-sports/

http://www.multiplemayhemmamma.com/2013/02/kids-and-sports.html

https://healthykidstoday.org/2018/02/02/stay-safe-playing-sports/

http://rockrivertimes.com/2015/06/10/to-excel-in-youth-sports-kids-need-couch-time/

https://www.activekids.com/parenting-and-family/articles/which-team-sport-should-your-kid-play

http://www.wholechildsports.com/2017/09/19/can-competitive-sports-affect-childs-friendships/

http://daviddewolf.com/do-you-hate-kids-sports-politics-these-3-tips-are-for-you/

https://www.activekids.com/soccer/articles/7-benefits-of-team-sports-for-kids

http://www.billfranklin.blog

https://drstankovich.com/smart-strategies-to-help-your-child-maximize-the-sport-experience/

https://nicershoes.com/best-running-shoes-for-kids-reviewed/

https://www.sportingschools.gov.au/news/More-to-kids-sport

https://www.cnn.com/2016/01/21/health/kids-youth-sports-parents/index.html

https://www.playkidssports.com/Kids-Sports.html

https://www.menshealth.com/trending-news/a19539121/kids-fitness/

http://www.momsteam.com/sports

http://www.kids-sports-activities.com/

https://www.daveramsey.com/blog/7-signs-kids-sports-taken-over-life-budget/

https://www.huffingtonpost.com/anne-josephson/15-reason-competitive-sports-are-great-for-kids-that-have-nothing-to-do-with-winning_b_7219150.html

https://www.consumerreports.org/digital-cameras-photography/how-to-shoot-great-sports-video-of-your-kids/

https://www.fatherly.com/play/best-sports-movies-for-kids/

https://www.parents.com/kids/safety/sports/things-parents-can-do-to-protect-sporty-kids-from-injuries/

Thank you for buying this book and reading it with your children!

Would you like to receive _free_ coloring pages of all the images in the book?

To get full-page drawings like the one below, totally free, just type this link into your browser: bit.ly/WinLosePages, and fill in the form.

The PDF will appear instantly in your browser.

Please consider leaving a short review on Amazon to tell others how you liked the book. Just go to bit.ly/WinLoseReviews.

Thanks! Happy Coloring!

... Bill Franklin

Made in the USA
Monee, IL
05 January 2020